MIDWAY

Also by Kayla Czaga

Dunk Tank
For Your Safety Please Hold On

MIDWAY

POEMS

KAYLA CZAGA

ANANSI

Published in Canada in 2024 and the USA in 2024 by House of Anansi Press Inc.
houseofanansi.com

28 27 26 25 24   1 2 3 4 5

Library and Archives Canada Cataloguing in Publication

Title: Midway / Kayla Czaga.
Names: Czaga, Kayla, author.
Description: Poems.
Identifiers: Canadiana (print) 20230533264 | Canadiana (ebook) 20230533272 |
ISBN 9781487012601 (softcover) | ISBN 9781487012618 (EPUB)
Classification: LCC PS8605.Z34 M53 2024 | DDC C811/.6—dc23

Cover image: Dave G. Kelly/Getty Images
Book design: Alysia Shewchuk

House of Anansi Press is grateful for the privilege to work on and create from the Traditional Territory of many Nations, including the Anishinabeg, the Wendat, and the Haudenosaunee, as well as the Treaty Lands of the Mississaugas of the Credit.

 Canada Council   Conseil des Arts   ONTARIO ARTS COUNCIL
for the Arts   du Canada   CONSEIL DES ARTS DE L'ONTARIO

With the participation of the Government of Canada
Avec la participation du gouvernement du Canada | Canadä

We acknowledge for their financial support of our publishing program the Canada Council for the Arts, the Ontario Arts Council, and the Government of Canada.

Printed and bound in Canada

CONTENTS

The Hairbrush / 3
I Go Back to November 1989 / 4
Metal Detecting / 6
Self-Portrait with Pizza Pop / 7
Pho Fish / 10
On Being Asked by a Former Professor If I Will
     Apply for That Teaching Gig / 12
Valentine's Day 2017 / 14
Macramé feat. Stevie Nicks / 15
Dear Brenda / 17
Emergency Exit / 19
Dad Movie / 21
The Peace Lily / 25
I Don't Want My Father to Live / 27
Anyone's Mother / 29
Safe Despair / 30
Plecostomus / 33
Side Effects / 34
Small Poem / 36
Painkiller / 37
The Midway / 38
The Power of Love / 39
Without Any Witches / 49
A Carefree Life / 50
I Have Never Written a Poem about My
     Father / 51
Another Poem about Dinosaurs / 53

The Smooth Dreamer / 55
The Sadness of Marge Simpson / 56
Freedom / 58
Father Christmas / 59
Static / 61
Dad Poem / 62
Produce / 66
Rules for Living / 67
Polyp / 69
Valentine's Day 2023 / 70
Baggage / 71
Coho / 72
Thirteen Years / 73
Winning / 75
I Long to Hear / 76
The Last Thing / 77

Acknowledgements / 79

MIDWAY

THE HAIRBRUSH

A few days after he died, my mother found it
in a drawer. Matted with white hair

it resembled an old man cactus
that had been meditating for centuries in the desert
or a mostly eaten cone of cotton candy.

From another angle, it was a giant cocoon
at the end of a lacquered branch.

Inside it a butterfly had been
knitting wings for sixty-six years.

Under other circumstances, it might've been mistaken
for a microphone generating its own static,
but there was nothing to say, no grand speeches

to be made because ultimately
it looked like nothing as much as what it was:
my dead father's hairbrush.

Here, she said, handing it to me,
Go grow yourself a new dad.

I GO BACK TO NOVEMBER 1989

After Sharon Olds

I see them in that shared hospital room—
my father shifting in the visitor chair, his fingers
twitching, he's craving a smoke, but is hopeful
they'll reach a decision before he goes;
my mother reclines on the thin twin bed, the legs
in front of her feel heavy, like bolts of fabric,
though the anaesthetic has almost worn off.
Tentatively she touches the bandages below
her bellybutton. Does she miss me in there?
Does the area ache? In an incubator down the hall
I am still building a set of lungs and can't ask
these questions. My imagination paints
the walls spearmint green, the linoleum pink
with a brown pattern. From behind a curtain,
a stranger's machine beeps like a metronome
marking off the minutes, hours—soon, days—
their daughter has lived without a name.
"Sarah?" my mother says, but before she's finished
the two syllables, my father shakes his head.
My mother crosses it off the list. I will not
be Sarah. Not Colleen. Not Lauren. Not Ashley.
Not Lucy with diamonds. Or wonderland Alice.
Unlike the parents in Olds's poem, these people
are not kids. They are not dumb. Or innocent.
They dated for a while, then broke up
and had other loves. In the late autumns
of their thirties, they met again and thought,
Sure, why not. I might be getting it wrong.
Maybe that's not exactly how it happened.
Still, they are old for first-time parents.
My father's hair is already brushed with grey;

I'll never remember it brown. Maybe they know
they'll get no second go at this naming business,
so they take their time. My father wanders outside
for his smoke, glances at me through a window
on his way. As the cold prairie air revives him,
does he consider how his daughter arrived
early and sudden as an ice storm, leaving
behind a quiet and glimmering aftermath?
And what is my mother thinking as a nurse
wheels me into the room so she can touch me
for the first time through a coaster-sized hole?
My father returns. My mother unfolds her list.
Runs her pencil down the remaining names.
They are patient. Maybe in this way they
are innocent. Like kids attempting to cross
a frozen lake, they go slow, dumb with the faith
that they could get this right if they watch
where they are going. If they tread carefully,
one step and then the next, they believe
they can make it safely to the other side.

METAL DETECTING

On a beach littered with tourists, my machine
beep-beeps above old foil ghosts,
above nickels, bolts, and toe rings.
I've been told of newer detectors
that can separate metal from metal,
distinguish wedding bands from Trojan wrappers,
and would tell me when to stick my fork
into sand, how deep to dig,
and when not to bother, to keep walking,
but this is my father's metal detector,
the one I watched him wave
over soccer fields and graveyards
while I strode a few feet behind,
his jockey—cutlery in my butt pockets,
a stainless steel smile. We filled a bucket
with old pennies I inherited sooner
than either of us expected and with it
this battery-operated divining stick.

Today the sea stretches out in front of me
like a tarp to lay my treasure on, the sand
bottomless, a burlap sack. *Beep beep*,
a beer tab. *Beep beep*, a nail. *Beep beep*,
my father, I can hear his sandals
slapping his heels and can almost
see him—*Beep beep*—kneeling down,
twirling the world with his old fork.

SELF-PORTRAIT WITH PIZZA POP

I put the Pizza Pop into the microwave.
I am fourteen years old. This morning was excruciating.
Of course I'm not really fourteen. I'm thirty-one.

Or seven. Or sixty-three. However I punch the numbers
into the microwave, I'm far away. At the same time,
I'm still fourteen, still crying in the kitchen.

See my purple hair, my pale fingers lifting the brown plate,
placing it at the centre of the microwave,
my nails painted with silver moons and stars

so someone might notice. But I sat alone all morning.
I wrote brilliant things in the margins of my coil notebooks
and no one noticed. Though the house is quiet

I imagine my classmates' distant laughter.
The Pizza Pop rotates like a jewelry-box ballet dancer.
The sky is low and crumpled as Saran Wrap.

The me who is nineteen and only five years ahead
hates the me in the kitchen, would beat her up at a bus stop
if she had the chance. She'd steal her wallet,

spit on her. But the me at thirty knows this girl's anger
is just deflected shame and pities us both.
A huge beige computer purrs in the living room,

I still believe it is filled with real friendship.
At any age, what I feel is real even if it does not exist.
Condensation drips from the underside of the sky

making fat grey puddles like portals in a children's epic—
somewhere I am still ten years old reading it.
A pantry filled with Ichiban, Cap'n Crunch, canned corn,

boxed stuffing, and Campbell's Chunky keeps me
alive. A freezer filled with spanakopita, Lean Cuisine,
and endless iterations of pizza keeps me alive.

I am kept alive by Taco Time Mexi-Fries and 7-Eleven coffee.
And I am still alive at Buffy's Diner, stacking
a pyramid of creamers and asking about the day's soup.

The microwave makes the sound of a levitating
spell book from a creepy fairy tale as it heats
my lunch with magic and carcinogens.

Half my age plus seven is the age that I am.
I am fourteen and believe my life will suck forever.
I am twenty-one and weeping in an abandoned

salmon cannery, slogging through *War and Peace*.
I am thirty and standing on a hotel balcony
repeating vows. I am nine and catching toads

in a plastic tobacco tin beside the stinky river.
I set the lid over the toads and whisper, *Goodnight, toads*.
The toads whisper, *Goodnight, milady*.

I imagine the Pizza Pop is filled with processed cheese,
sauce and small chunks of sausage
the way it always is, but I can't know this for certain.

It could be empty, a manufacturing error.
Or maybe it is filled with a silver moon and metal stars.
Maybe it contains every age of me, all snuggled

up inside the yellow sleeping bag of dough.
Maybe the microwave will melt these girls together,
meld them into one consistent self—

if that's the case, I should've set a longer timer.
Inside a Pizza Pop, a god may be building a new world
with no people in it, only talking animals

who never say anything interesting. They sing hymns
of praise beneath a yellow pastry moon, cheese stars.
They pray for day but it is always butter-scented

twilight. The Pizza Pop spins and spins
like the girl who was cursed to dance herself
to death. The computer's screen saver gyrates.

The microwave's timer counts down: Ten. Nine.
I am eight years old, feeling shame for the first time
changing in a pool change room. I am seven, six.

I am five years old and these are my first-day-of-school
shoes, my sparkly name pencils. I am four, three.
I am two when I press the button. The cow says, Moo.

The cow says, *Got Milk?* The cow says, *Who do you
think you could be?* The cow says, *Three ... Two ...*
The microwave emits a three-toned chime.

The spell is broken. By the time school lets out
the sky will be dark as the inside of a Pizza Pop.
I will walk home alone. I will microwave dinner.

The evening will be moonless, starless
beneath the quiet dough of clouds.

The saddest creature on earth
bobs in a foggy tank
in that Vietnamese restaurant
on the corner of Main & 33rd.
He—maybe not *he*, though
I think of the fish that way—
has my father's face, his exact
features, but the colouring's
wrong. My father was ruddy;
this fish is translucent and grey.
Otherwise it's him. I'd know
those lips and that nose
on any creature. I wish I could say
he's the reason I'm here,
but it's the soup I go for.
And the indifferent service.
Floating in his cold broth,
my father greets every guest.
The door opens and he opens
his mouth. Closes it. Blinks.
A paper sign discourages
tapping his glass. My soup arrives
in a bowl larger than my head
and no one asks if I like it,
if I need anything, no one
says anything except the radio
overhead chanting top 40s,
pimpled by ads. And you
want to know why my father is sad,
the saddest creature on earth?
Surely, you must wonder,
isn't there an endangered turtle
or penguin with alopecia

more deserving of the title?
The fish with my father's face
opens his mouth but no sound
passes through the glass.
He breathes his own waste's
foul weather. Watching
strangers eat, he gulps at
uniform food pellets.
With shadows from outside
swimming across her face,
his daughter eats alone
at the table by the window.
The pieces of our grief are
numerous as his new scales
and the noodles in my soup
sending up a curtain of steam.
I sip the complicated broth
of my father's sadness, beg
his scales for forgiveness
as they weigh me.

ON BEING ASKED BY A FORMER PROFESSOR IF I WILL
APPLY FOR THAT TEACHING GIG

Teacher, I reject your lecture on sparrows.
I have read seven hundred Romantic poems
and all I learned was how to flirt with lakes.
I dialed your private line and babbled
about thesis formatting into the beep abyss.
Guiding my delete button with a bouquet
of pronouns and a bowl of dried mangosteen,
you encouraged my river metaphors
until I admitted the river was just an iridescent
byproduct from the aluminum smelter.
When the salmon beached, their gills strung
with microbeads, I did not relocate to Toronto
as you suggested. I fled academia to pursue
a more authentic handshake. I found work
in a bar named after a card game named after
a bar. I welcomed the articles. I had abstractions
tattooed onto my pen arm. I plucked a fly
from a jug of beer and delivered the jug
to the customer. I quit the committee
for approving the committee's minutes.
Instead I wanted to suck the red out
of the redhead and wander in a colour fever.
Wanted to add *happy hour* to my syllabus.
Wanted an entire life on airplane mode.
When the customer tried to buy my body
with balmy money I kept my eye turned upwards
like an explorer guided home by Polaris.
I drank the beer and in so doing
drank the tiny urines of fruit flies.
I shook cocktails that resembled spring run-off
after writing *bitumen* over and over
on my serving notepad, not knowing

what to make of anything, waking daily
with tear ducts clogged with tarsand.
You attended graduation ceremonies
at the burning academy you love—
an ember in red robes. For a while
I sent lukewarm queries and edited my CV.
I reread your tender notes on the thesis
I failed to complete   you saw a future
for me that I couldn't envision
in our choking world and our shrinking field.
For a while, the lights across the harbour
blinked on and off like a helpful line
of Morse code in a middle-grade mystery novel,
but by the time I walked out of the bar,
they'd stopped. The far shore was dark.

The waterfall at Manoa
doesn't think about what it's doing
with its life. It simply falls.
We hiked all afternoon
through hot rain to gawk at it,
two obvious tourists.
Our sandals in the mud
made the wet sounds
of sucking on chicken wings.
On that chocolate holiday
of *Will You Be Mine* we hiked
among glossy tropical leaves
up a Hawaiian mountain
in the hopes we might learn
something about falling.
When I return to that day
in my mind, I still feel
the cinnamon-heart heat
of my sunburnt shoulders,
and your heat radiating
next to me like a shot
of good whisky.
How brave and true
and stupid and beautiful
that waterfall looked,
rushing up to the edge,
then plunging on
past it forever.

MACRAMÉ feat. STEVIE NICKS

Over cake she isn't supposed to eat and wine
she isn't supposed to drink, my mother tells me
about all the things she macraméd before I was born.
Of course, I remember the owl tacked onto
the basement wall until she got sick of it,
its wooden eyes big as my kid fists, but I don't recall
the planters she insists dangled in the kitchen
brimming with waxy lilies and orchids.
She made a vest for her friend who died
and a kind of floating side table for her other friend,
the one she fell out with. Because it's Mother's Day
I don't nag her about the wine or the cake
and I listen as she lists objects I'll never see:
a wall hanging for my grandmother up north,
star key chains, welcome mat, swing.
In my mind I can see her driving to Craft Land
in her old Camaro with oversized sunglasses
and a perm, heaping the backseat with hemp and beads,
Stevie Nicks looping though the stereo.
And would you believe me if I told you
she macraméd Stevie Nicks too, that my mother's
hands measured and wove that diva's thick voice,
unspooled feathers and hair, snipped
the white-winged dove from the fine skylark,
would you understand what I'm trying to mean?
If I say my mother macraméd all of Idaho,
can you begin to feel the horizon as a hairy string,
the potatoes beaded so deep into the earth
you dig them up baked? She macraméd
the world's largest scorpion and the world's
smallest goat. She macraméd a fishbowl so tight
it never leaked. Then she macraméd me.
Her right hand steering the fork through

her wedge of cake is still agile despite the arthritis—
fingers tapered, nails long and lacquered.
You knot the strings one way for a rectangle,
she says, and the other forms an endless spiral.

DEAR BRENDA

In the bottle that washed up on the beach
instead of a note I found
my father's false teeth

smashed into pieces
like pills for me to swallow.

They fell from the bottle single file,
shiny airplane passengers
evacuating via the emergency slide

and I scattered them in the sand for seagulls
to pick at like popcorn kernels.

The sky was grey. The sand was darker grey.
The sea was darker still
with flecks of green between its teeth.

I walked for a while and found
a second bottle with a note in it

intended for someone else.
Dear Brenda ... it began, so I stuffed it
back into its bottle, back into sand.

Seagulls heckled the morning's sorry performance.
I found a fourth bottle, which was empty.

Among a beached otter's garbled guts,
I found a fifth bottle containing the otter's bladder
shrivelled like an old *Get Well Soon* balloon.

I chose not to mention the third bottle
whose note was meant for me alone.

Oh god, I thought, will this beach go on
forever, bottle after bottle,
some filled with sand,

some with distant sighs
we'll convince ourselves are the sea.

One bottle coughed up enough change
for me to catch a bus and ride
as far away as I could want.

I found a sixth and a seventh bottle.
I found the jawbone of a baby whale.

My fingers were getting cold.
I thought of my note, now confetti for the crabs.
It told me my dad was sorry for going away.

I didn't believe it and vowed to find
the note that proved otherwise

while the sea went on sucking lozenges,
cooling her fevered head
with salt-water-filled beer bottles.

I picked my way among piles of driftwood
which resembled the detritus

of some great wreckage
I knew would take me a very long time
to sort through and reassemble.

When I was twenty, I worked as a tour guide
in an abandoned salmon cannery.
Before that, I sold Payless shoes. Years later,
between midnight and six a.m. three days a week
I faced cans of chickpeas, Campbell's, and Canada Dry
in a closed Thrifty Foods with Luke
who carried up the aisles with him a ghetto blaster
that blasted sexist radio shows and Led Zeppelin.
I went on to email feedback to aspiring writers
I'd never meet, paying excessive attention
to their adjectives. I made blue cocktails
for college kids. I took a poet's papers
out of a dozen Rubbermaid bins, sorted them
into chronological order, stacked them back in,
and shipped the bins to London, Ontario.
Because I signed an NDA, I can't admit to writing
segments of a mystery story Neil Patrick Harris loved,
but I can talk about the dinosaur erotica.
I rode around in a rental van with Brian
telling northern kids it was ok
if they didn't know what they wanted to be
when they grew up, though they'd be grownups
by now and I wonder what they went on to be
and if they remember me at all.
I told Lenny to quit teasing my servers.
I picked Gala apples. I picked Suncrisp apples.
I picked McIntosh apples in a gentle and specific way
because they bruise so easily. I made no-foam
matcha lattes. I ordered too many cases of house wine.
I helped Rhea retire. I wore a headset backstage
and whispered to the Ukrainian dancing girls
that they were up next on the telethon.
For all these jobs, I made money. Enough to live on,

amounts that always felt like too much or too little
compensation for the tasks I'd performed.
Like the one afternoon I did nothing
but glue labels onto cans of salmon
because the boss forgot about me in the office.
Or that time I got so lost in the back
of the Thrifty Foods that I ran out the emergency exit
and walked around the entire store.
I took my time, peeking into the windshield of
a broken-down murder van and snapping photos
with my phone of the shopping carts
lit up by streetlights and their own reflections
off puddles. That's what the apocalypse will look like
in case you've ever wondered: shining abandoned
shopping carts on cracked asphalt.
It was a little past three in the morning.
I was so cold and so tired I thought
I'd be there, in that parking lot, forever
and it's possible a part of me still is. Then I banged
on the front doors until Luke let me back in.

DAD MOVIE

In the movie, a secret agent and a marine biologist
must pair up to save the world from a sea monster

the villains have engineered into an organic weapon.
The villains might be Russians, anarchists, neo-Nazis,

or terrorists. The movie doesn't linger on identity,
insisting evil is eternal and interchangeable.

My father pours an Old Style pilsner into his beer mug
as I pull a Calgary Flames afghan across my lap

and crinkle open a bag of Old Dutch salt'n'vinegar.
We've seen this one before. The marine biologist

and secret agent don't want to work together.
He's hot-headed; she's a snob. Both of them tend

to their backstories as if dredging up rusty old crab traps.
If the movie was directed by Michael Bay, her button-up

will come undone beyond our suspension of disbelief
and the hero will ripple under his trench coat, his bicep

dwarfing her torso, echoing the monster of the deep.
My father clicks the volume up to cover my mother's

upstairs coughing. In this version, he and I are the sea
monsters, lurking below. His afghan is patterned

with wolves and mountain ranges. If the movie
was directed by Clint Eastwood, the secret agent

will have a lost daughter who will surface like flotsam
halfway through the plot. Misunderstanding their filial banter

the marine biologist will recoil into herself
like a hermit crab. The sea monster also has a daughter who—

with biological urgency—will carry out her father's work
once our heroes have blown him up. She will be much

harder to kill. Her eggs will be lethal and legion.
Sound pushes through our floorboards: the dishwasher

being emptied and reloaded, plates clattering
into cupboards. When I leave for the bathroom, my father

presses pause, pours another Pilsner, and relaxes into
the brown floral sofa that pretty much sums up my childhood.

If this was a Scorsese movie, there'd be no marine biologist,
no women at all, no monster except the one that slithers

inside each man, as my father drives home at dawn
from the smelter with the other busted-up family men.

All of this happened a long time ago.
Cigarette smoke curled above his head like tentacles.

His beer mug had a wooden handle and little flowers
etched into its amber body. If his life was a movie,

the mug would mean something, Wes Anderson kitschy,
but we donated it to a thrift store in Parksville.

Once the movie ended, I would touch the artifacts
on my father's shelves and think *staging*, wonder

what the ammolite shell, the hula-girl bust,
or the medical compendium revealed about his character.

Like a couple of engineered plants that grow best
in blue light, we repeated this ritual most weekends.

A close-up of the ocean. Pan out to a treeline, research station,
two kids in the sand constructing a palace with a bucket.

Something disturbs the water's surface. Cut to:
the marine biologist lifting a vial filled with dark liquid.

The secret agent asks, "So, that'll kill it?"
"It'll draw the evil out of it," she assures him.

A green telephone rings. Upstairs, my mother would be
watching home improvement shows in a home

that would never improve, but settle into its rot
like a shipwreck. Its roof and windows weathered

the weather best as could be expected given
the conditions. The conditions: the marine biologist

looks up from her paperwork to see the secret agent
heaving an old lady onto the life raft and falls

immediately in love. But the secret agent
has been in love with her since the movie started

forty-seven minutes ago, having kept his feelings
sheathed in one-liners and macho responsibility.

With renewed energy and a rosy complexion,
the marine biologist completes her work.

Of course my mother would be the marine biologist,
studying us under her microscope with scientific remove.

In the movie, my father punches a wall because
he loves her, goddamnit, and his emotional expression

is limited by Hollywood gender and early-2000s
special effects. A speedboat explodes. A seaplane explodes.

A submarine explodes. And I, their sea monster,
evil and beloved, wave one loopy tentacle

before my great eye goes glassy. During the credits,
my father would ask how school was going

and try to indoctrinate me on politics. Sometimes
he'd show me a photo album from his own youth,

which contained no movies, only staticky farmland.
Or he'd say nothing, just shuffle over to the television,

open up the DVD player, and put in the sequel.

THE PEACE LILY

The peace lily I bought
at Thrifty Foods for $4.99
taught me something
about beauty. When I saw
its poker-green leaves
and flowers, like studded
Jacobsen Egg Chairs,
I rushed it into my cart,
wheeled to the till, carried
it home, and centred it
atop a sunny bookshelf.
Within a week, its leaves
had black spots. A second
week saw its flowers drop.
My mother-in-law said
it needed repotting
and took it—returned it
in a larger pot, trimmed
of rot. Still, it withered.
The internet told me to
shield it from breezes,
to mist it, fertilize,
and comb for mites. I did
everything, and as a reward,
it sent out one new flower,
alive as a child's hand,
which drooped before
ever really blooming.
To say the peace lily died
would be an understatement.
Like a famous connoisseur
of death, it took its time:
every last leaf withered

into a black ash that stuck
to the shelf, and what
remained in the pot
resembled the dregs
of a great forest fire.
I am not someone
who if you smashed all
her mirrors or splattered
her canvases with tar
would suffer very much,
but I had admired
the lily and hoped
it would thrive.
Yet the more I did for it
the less interested
it seemed in living,
and in the end—tipping it
into my compost bin—
a bit of me loved
being done with it.

I DON'T WANT MY FATHER TO LIVE

if he is dead. If my father is dead I want
him to be dead, not living on
in my memories, flickering
in and out like sparrows
from under cars in parking lots.
This afternoon I almost asked my mother
to put him on the phone, wanted
to talk to him about all the new trailers
for blockbuster movies.
When I sit alone on my sofa at night
my father tells me about his birdhouses
and he doesn't listen (not that he did
when he lived) to me tell him
that he is dead and the birds refuse to live
in those houses because he nailed
them too close together.
He died believing spring
would hatch quick-winged families
in his yard and that his DVD player
would open to accept
the new superhero movie like a child
extending her hand for a candy.
Once I saw him reach out
exactly like that and a robin floated down
from a chalk-coloured sky
to remove a breadcrumb from his lifeline.
"See," he'd said. "Birds just like me."
Had he lived, his backyard
would be filled with birds
and he would step down
from his porch, their funny prophet
with long white feathers and sweatpants.
Had he lived, robins would clip

their claws to his t-shirt and lift him
into the sky, slow as end credits
scrolling up the screen.
Only he didn't live
and this isn't a movie.

ANYONE'S MOTHER

Morning moves like marmalade
on toast—sweet, yes, but sticky. Some lumps.
My student's emailed to tell me he's done
with his name, wants to publish
under a new one and could I—
would I—rename him? I've never
wanted to be anyone's mother.
In my building's parking lot, sparrows nest
between the spikes intended to deter them
and someone might take this to mean
nature always finds a way, but all I can think of
is the discomfort of motherhood.
For my sister-in-law, pregnant
with her first-born, every chair
was a triumph of hostile architecture.
What would I—could I—call my student,
a man I hardly knew? It's a task
impossible as naming a fetus
I haven't met or counting potatoes
by inspecting the plant's visible leaves.
I would like to call him "The Student
Formerly Known as Demanding,"
but could settle for Potato, or Peter,
Milton, Marmalade, or The Speaker.
I should call him Sparrow
because I want him to thrive
despite his emails and the spikes,
I bet he doesn't see those yet.
He's envisioning words—his own—
printed in a book as tenderly as a mother
hand-stitches a name tag
into her son's orange windbreaker.

Because she could not stop for Death,
Death drove alongside, shouting—
Emily, get in the car.

Death said Emily seemed older, closer to his age.

When Death slid into Emily's DMs, did he send:
    a) threats
    b) eggplant emojis
    c) obscure Slovenian poetry
    d) links to news articles
        in which he featured prominently
    e) grim reaper tattoos with,
        How about my face on your bicep, baby?
        Just you'n'me and Immortality.

Death said Emily was different.
Emily said that was so *Death.*
Their conversations went: *Death,*
Death, Death, Death, metal, Death.

For their one-month anniversary
Death bought Emily a birch-white box,
five and a half feet long with pewter knobs.

Emily's journal entries went: Death—
Death—Death—Death—Homework—Death.

Death tutored Emily in physics.
For instance, if Death dropped Emily off
the steeple, he could calculate
whether the impact would snap her neck.

Death knew all about things like physics,
obscure knots, nu metal, and what living
girls were like, what they liked.

Death said dead girls didn't understand him.
Only Emily could understand him.

Only Emily and her metres of lace,
museum of ceramic feelings, her breath
flogging the pane and long, trembling
fingers could understand him.

Late at night over the phone, Death read
a poem to Emily that made her bones glow.

On weekends she visited the hospital cafeteria
where he spooned corn and wore a hairnet.
She ate Jell-O and acted incurable.

Death said there were opportunities
for him in the city. He drove off
in a button-down and black denim.

Emily stared out into the peppy blue Amherst light,
which only understood different forks
and how to hold them. It made her tired.
In her notebook, she wrote, D+E 4eva
&eva—and meant it.

Death got hired doing security at a bank,
buzzed his head, bought a tie and looked alive.

He said, *I am lifting weights now.*
I am feeling so powerful.

He said, *Our connection*
is too special for monogamy.

Emily's journal entries went: Death—Death—
Death—Emily—see I am doing better—
Death—soon I will be ok—Death—
Death + Emily—Death – Emily =
I will never understand physics so long
as I live—Death. Amherst blows.

Death said, *I'll visit next weekend,* as weekends
piled up in pages on Emily's desk,
and she circled *all of the above* on every test.

Emily believed her breathing would take
forever to get normal. She made horizontal
marks in the margins of her arms,

folded her notebook pages into coffins
and cranes until she felt a formal
purple purging throughout her veins.

PLECOSTOMUS

Of all the critters we kept
in that murky aquarium, she was the one
I loved most, that name alone a point in her favour.

Unlike those flashy guppies and neons
or the snails with no apparent faces
who hung like fungal toenails

on the tropical backdrop, she had real style.
Leopard-printed and fringed
in an Elizabethan collar, her drag name

was Cat Suckermouth.
For days she'd evade me, lounging
in the ceramic castle or tucked

under the duckweed until she re-emerged
to french-kiss the fingertip
I pressed to the glass so hard

it turned the same
intimate pink as her mouth
and flickered with my pulse.

She ate her tank-mates' waste
and when they died, she ate them too,
outliving all others

and, ultimately, our interest.
We flushed her. But I've seen her since
in sewers, a fierce little cemetery,

my floating resilience seminar,
she persists. Every gutter, puddle,
and bathtub: her runway.

This gallery is too bright for a poetry reading
and you feel constipated, which always happens
after you've flown. The walls display photos
of modular eco-homes. The theme of this event
is social justice and you can't decide what to read,
don't consider yourself a "social justice" poet
though the festival has selected you to be here,
in this mid-sized Canadian city in mid-February.
From his van, your volunteer pointed out the river,
the arty street—its coffee shop and vegan restaurant.
Your knees quiver behind the podium, the way
they always do, only this time a little more
as you read what you have: poems about being a girl,
not believing "being a girl" holds its weight
alongside natural disasters, coups, and genocides,
that your body holds its weight. You're shaky
and bloated. You want to go home, but you fill
the ten minutes the festival is paying you for.
When it's over, another reader approaches to ask you
how many of your friends have offed themselves.
Of course he doesn't say it like this. He says,
"Was suicide a problem?" the way a scientist
might, like suicide is an unpleasant side effect
of northern living while adolescent and female,
akin to acne and clumpy mascara. You turn
towards him, this earnest teacher from Ontario
who read poems about the Middle East because
he did a year somewhere. Now he's asking you
about fourteen-year-olds yanked from bathtubs
in beach towels. He's curious about pill-poppers,
wrist-slitters, bleach-guzzlers, though he
doesn't say this exactly. He mentions an article.
Shakes his head. Calls it "an epidemic."

As he waits, your mind pinballs over responses
he isn't looking for: the hundred consecutive
days you journalled about killing yourself,
or your best friend telling your mother her burns
were from pulling pizzas from ovens. Or maybe
he does want to know. Maybe he does care.
Maybe you're being unkind to this awkward stranger
but you can't help yourself, knowing the bodies
in his poems are not bodies he ever touched,
not bodies he slept beside when his own was still
strange and new to him. You smile at the poet.
You sip your wine. You imagine it careening through
your body like a southbound rust bucket. Inside
sit two girls. The driver taps the wheel to a song
that rhymes with her mood while the passenger,
both feet on the dash, watches the blur of trees,
more world than she's ever seen. She likes poetry,
sure, it's alright, but what she really needs is
gas money and sandwiches, a room for the night.

SMALL POEM

The closest thing I have to a heritage
is a photograph of my grandmother
being fake-arrested in a fake saloon
in Arizona. Two cowboy actors aim
plastic pistols at her. She's laughing
in the photo, my grandmother,
in cowboy boots and a ten-gallon hat,
her face thrown back to the rafters.
When anyone says, *I heard she shot
her husband,* her sons chorus,
Which one? Four-foot-eight and she
wielded every inch. In her left hand,
she crumpled the word *orphan*
like a napkin and belched into it.
In her right hand: vodka and gifts.
The colours of her flag are identical
to the colours of flags from many
other countries. The colours of her
sweatpants are bargain-bin bright.
And the colours of her flag are
I'm going to count to three and
[no translation available] and *Go
tie back your hair so I can see
your beautiful face.*

PAINKILLER

I put his ashes on the dog beach
I put his ashes on my bookshelf
I paid a company to put his ashes
inside a glass paperweight
I put his ashes off a cliff in Ucluelet
I put his ashes in the soil of my Norfolk pine
I put his ashes on a windowsill
of the Medicine Hat Best Western
I put his ashes inside a dream I had
I put his ashes onto a dollar bill
I put his ashes onto a second dollar bill
I put a dollar bill filled with his ashes
into a slot machine in Las Vegas
I put his ashes in a pond of greedy carp
I put his ashes onto a plate so I could
transfer them into an empty Advil bottle
Daddict Dadvil I put my dad's ashes
into my mouth and swallowed

Finally there's a small bottle
that will solve all my problems, my father thought.
And he wasn't wrong—it's impossible to have problems

when you're dead. Busted from decades of night shifts,
his body was an obsolete mill in a shuttered boom town,
and finally there was a small bottle

a magician had conjured from behind my father's right ear:
pills like clown cars to carry him far from
his problems. It was impossible for anything to be wrong

with Ferris Wheel pupils lifting him up,
offering views of the river far beyond his failed industry.
Finally there was a small bottle

my father could shoot at to win himself
the softest top-shelf prize, the hugest blue elephant.
Impossibly, for once, he had no problems, nothing wrong—

no pain, no insomnia, no mortgage, no shame, the midway
had arrived for my father, so he could just drink
(finally there was a small bottle)
and not be wrong inside impossible problems.

THE POWER OF LOVE

In Bloemfontein, South Africa
where I was speaking
at an arts festival
sixteen thousand kilometres away
from the town I grew up in,
I heard a band covering
"The Power of Love."
Between events I was wandering
through an outdoor market
looking for souvenirs
when the first bars rang out
like a long distance phone call.
I sat down on a rectangle
of grass and ate shawarma.
A man who resembled
my father walked by
wearing khaki shorts
and swaying like drunken wheat.
Father, I wanted to say,
Sit down. Eat with me.
I wanted to call a stranger
father while my own father
occupied a tube-shaped urn
on my desk at home.
The lyrics grew
into a dramatic lather
that floated over
to where I was sitting
and it would've been easy
to just let it power wash
the grief from my heart.
Many people have given
me advice since he died.

Maybe even you.
Yes, you. You who are
reading this now.
Maybe you were
very sorry for my loss.
Maybe you said,
Your grief is Lake Michigan
on a map of time. Or:
He is with you always,
your father. He's a pattern,
a chemical reaction
that lights up the EEG
like a Christmas tree.
Sitting in Bloemfontein,
my body blasted by time change,
Canada calling to me,
I could've almost believed
there was meaning in it.
But I don't consider suffering
a class people can take
for self-improvement.
My father is not a part
of my grey matter
where memory skips stones
out onto the gushy surface
of Nostalgia Lake.
My father is not
a door to unlock.
I can't step on through him.
He's dead—I checked.

*

Less than a week later
I would be standing in London
in the Tate Modern

watching a video art installation
of a woman lowering
her feet into a bowl of blood
then pacing the streets
of Guatemala City.
At regular intervals she placed
alternating soles
into her metal bowl and kept going.
I wonder how long she walked—
the recording is fifty-nine minutes.
I watched her while tourists churned
in many languages through
the gallery around me.
Then I looked at the Kandinsky,
at Jenny Holzer's hallway of quotes,
and several B-side Picassos.
Then I looked at my wife
and said, *I want a sandwich.*
Maybe I meant ham.
Maybe I meant simple
comfortable carbohydrates
to remind me of home.
Home, where a property
management company
keeps ripping out our floors
and our cat knocks
between rooms in the plastic cone
she's velcroed into to stop her
from chewing up her feet.
I named her Grandpa
because we got her
a few weeks after my father died,
but didn't realize that was why
until months later.
I thought I just liked the name.
Slow emotional jet lag.

My whole life rotating
before me like a column
of shawarma meat.
Little tube of ashes
resembling a kaleidoscope—
what would I see
if I could peer through it?
The suitcase he carried to Canada—
small as a shoebox—
propped up on my desk
like a bit of immigrant kitsch.
His Calgary Flames coffee mug.
His empty poker wallet.
My shitty dead father
art installation.
The Tate Modern, sitting
on the riverbank, giving
London the brick finger.
Us sitting between the Tate
and the Thames—a little drunk,
a little jet-lagged and in love.

*

In April in a beige train car
in Southern Ontario, I read
Sally Rooney's second novel,
all of it in one nauseating gulp
and I'm the only one I know
who doesn't wish
for a different ending.
Let your characters be
complicated and miserable,
novelists—god knows
it's how I've felt often enough
even in London, England,

seeing things I'd dreamed of
because my feet were swollen
double from the heat.
It's something that's only started
in the last year or two—
the swelling, not the misery.
(Everyone who knows me
knows how prone I am
to being totally miserable.)
In that beige train car
in Southern Ontario I realized
I would never be Sally Rooney,
never be very young
and very famous.
That station passed ages ago.
With a plastic ham sandwich
I watched the last
of my youth vanish
behind working-class hills.
The last of my youth
looked just like another Tim Hortons,
which serves burgers now,
as well as the same people
it has always served,
my father and me.
You can't spell human
without h a m, is something
I once tweeted.
As is, *It's obvious why*
we call money "tender."
A poet I admire followed me back
on Twitter and unfollowed me
a couple of weeks later.
I can't say I blame him,
but it hit me right
in the daddy issues.

Then I walked into a room
of Rothkos and found my wife
hating Rothko so perfectly
I almost couldn't argue with her.
But of course I did.
She who will meet me anywhere,
and even used up her Air Miles
to fly to London
and stand with me in rooms
of art and hold my hand.
Most days it seems impossible
I have loved someone this long,
screaming, *I am your lady*
and you are my woman,
at her as she weaves us
through semis on the I-5
to some conference or other.
It's why I need Rothko
and all of his gooey purple blues.
It's why hotel rooms
and Celine Dion power
ballads were invented.

*

For Valentine's Day
we flew to Las Vegas
and she watched me rub
my father's ashes into
American dollar bills and feed
those American dollar bills
into slot machines—
the bills were rejected
then accepted with a waterfall
of sound effects—
watched me flip his ashes

into fountains on copper
American pennies.
Trump Hotel sat at the edge
of our sightline
like a fat gold tombstone.
That was the week
Celine wasn't playing Vegas,
so we went to the Backstreet Boys
whose backup dancers
danced better than the boys
themselves because—no matter
how much they are loved—
even nineties heartthrobs turn forty
and throw out their backs
trying to get down, get down
and move it all around.
Time's the greatest hit, boys.
She piggybacked me back
to our hotel room
in fake New York, my feet
two inflated pool floaties of pain,
and laid me down on a duvet
patterned with skyscrapers.
Was that before or after
I threw myself off
the fake Brooklyn Bridge?
Before I drank a metre-long
margarita and we watched
Hoarders all night.
Before we drove to Portland
for a conference but after
I went to Parksville
to visit my mother, who
may never approve of us.
I go away so often I worry
she'll leave me, but going away

is my job. Going away
and having feelings
and writing them all down
is my job. As is standing
in rooms and reading
my feelings out loud
to strangers. My wife's job
is replacing old windows
in people's homes,
switching them out
for newer windows
with better insulation.
On my more miserable days
I believe only one of us
is helping people see
the world and it isn't me.

*

In June this poem dreamed
it was invited to speak inside
an Anne Carson poem
and given a bus ticket
to Hades, a decent per diem.
Then I woke up, neck tweaked
from the ancient Greyhound seat,
crumpling it somewhat.
Hades was just a gas station,
a bar with a sign proclaiming
untended minors would
have their skeletons leashed
to Cerberus, a busted
VLT machine, a barmaid
named Magda who pointed
the way to my dad's—
Tell him to come pay his tab.

I followed a tidy row
of tent trailers
alongside a river I assumed
would be filled with ghosts,
but when I strode closer
it was filled like a regular river
with water and garbage—
shoes, car parts, Celine Dion CDs.
When I found my father, he was just
tending a little flower patch
and seemed—finally—ok.
He looked up at me over
his darkly glowing stargazers
and set his spade down,
so he could show me
a special moss. Orange alfalfa,
beaded with mercury;
it grows from memories.
Then he led me
into his little camper
and poured me a beer
the colour of 1997.
You can drink this, he said,
but better not eat anything.
He turned on his television.
I wished him a happy Father's Day
and asked him why
he had to go away.
He squinted out through
his kitchen window
as if it was a kaleidoscope, glowing
with all the busted-up
bits of his life swirling
together as weather—
a song that played and played
on the radio for sixty-six years,

a hit the artist was sick
of singing. He saw all of it
and said, *Shit happens.*
Maybe he meant his death.
Maybe he meant root rot
in the underworld.
Maybe he meant life is a series
of people you have
to learn how to leave
or sometimes you take a cow
to the market and come back
with a palmful of pomegranate seeds,
and no daughter.
He could've meant anything
but I want to believe
he was trying to say,
Sometimes I am frightened
but I'm ready to learn
of the power of love.

WITHOUT ANY WITCHES

In my hometown, beside the old motel—
at least when I lived there—was this sheet of plywood
held upright by two-by-fours staked into the grass.
On the front of it a family had been painted:
one painted man and one painted woman
beside otherwise identical but shorter figures,
their son and daughter. They all wore black—
ankle-length dresses for the women, greatcoats
for the men with centre-ironed trousers.
I liked best the gold buckles on their boots,
even the women's boots had these. Eight gold buckles.
On the men's heads were straw hats and the women
wore bonnets, except none of them had faces,
these had been sawn out, leaving four ovals
in the painting through which trees glared,
or, from a different angle, asphalt. It reminded me
of a play the local theatre troupe liked doing,
The Crucible, only without any witches.
In places the paint had begun to wear away
so you could see wood grain through the son's boots,
and the graffiti on the daughter's apron
that had been covered up with the wrong white,
the sprayed-on body part poking through.
There were three ways to drive downtown
and two of them took you by this wooden family.
In any weather they stood there, like the pro-lifers
in gumboots and parkas outside the pink hospital.
In my hometown (though I don't know why
I call it that, having never felt at home there)
you could go to the old motel and stand
behind that family, put your face into one
of the ovals and it became their face.
If you did that, there was never any shortage
of proud locals willing to take your photo.

A CAREFREE LIFE

My father went to bed one night five years ago
and the sleeping pills worked so good, they're still working.

Last July, a redhead named Michelle emptied
four Costco-sized syringes into my mother's IV line.

Like a couple going to the movies, my parents
entered their efficient pharmaceutical deaths

bored but curious, as if the events were happening
to fictional strangers in some far-off place.

You will have a carefree life,
my mother's final fortune cookie read

and I still keep the slip of paper
in my wallet though the fate isn't mine.

Instead, the hangover wears my body like that
awkward alien from *Men in Black,*

demanding sugar and water, as two Tylenol
dissolve going down. I lift the remote.

I change the channel but the same rerun
is playing on every station. I feel like the crud

I accidentally touch sometimes, whatever it is
that collects under cushions on my couch.

asleep on the toilet. I have never described him
folded forward like an airplane safety card's illustration
of brace position or slumped against the tank
with his head tipped back and dentures slipping
off his gums. I have never confessed how much
I wanted to wedge a finger into that dark gap
between my father and his fake teeth just to see
what it would feel like. I could feel the cement
under the carpet though I've never written a poem
about how my feet were cold for seventeen years.
I've never compared the polio vaccine scar
on his shoulder to a carp's bloodless mouth or claimed
the freckles dotting his back were villages on a map
of that dissolved Soviet state he came from.
I've never recorded how it would happen at any
time of day, especially in the afternoon, as daylight
curled in his lap like a cat and black sweatpants
pooled around his ankles like a faulty portable hole
to a dimension where this never happened.
I've never admitted in a poem that the reason
my father fell asleep on the toilet was because
he'd worked graveyard shifts for so many years
that regular sleep had died in him and it was only
zombie sleep he could have at that point,
gobbling up his brains when he didn't see it coming.
I probably don't need to explain that he worked
these shifts for my mother and me, so that we could eat
and go shopping. I've never written about opening
the bathroom door and seeing my father so still
I believed for longer than a moment that he had died
until his ribcage finally bloomed and I could
breathe too. I've never described how similar
and different it was to finding him in his bed,

but not realizing until after I had touched him
that time he was really dead. And I've especially never
written a poem about his fear when I woke him
or what he saw in those moments he stared before
he could see me, when I could tell he wasn't seeing
his daughter. A fear there are no pills for. A fear
metaphors fail. My father braced for impact.

ANOTHER POEM ABOUT DINOSAURS

Recently while reading my dinosaur erotica poem
at a festival, I thought, *Is this it?* Is this the life
I wanted when I was a child? To grow up to tell
the world's longest dinosaur dick joke
to rooms full of strangers? Well, no. Of course not.
Though it's true I loved dinosaurs and often
visualized their bones deep below me in the earth
wherever I walked, my thoughts were not sexual.
Mostly I wanted to stop wearing those awful sweaters
with appliqué cats and collars my mother brought
home for me from Northern Reflections. I wanted,
if I'm honest, to be smarter than anyone. I wanted
a journal with a lock but when I got one I wrote in it
only once, recording in my best third-grade cursive:
   This Book Belongs to Kayla Czaga.
Whenever I said something embarrassing
I wanted to switch schools or sail to Antarctica
to study penguins slip'n'sliding on milky green ice.
I wanted the precious Long John in the dozen,
my own private Narnia, days-of-the-week socks,
and the indefinite cancellation of gym class.
Every Friday, wearing Friday socks, I wanted
to bring the winning item in to show and tell,
to finally best Kevin King's silkworm collection.
So one Friday I brought in the rock my father
found in the dirt near Drumheller—an ancient shell
curled up like a cinnamon bun—extracted it
from my backpack and held it up so the light
would glimmer across its iridescent hull. But then
no one said anything. No one cared about a thing
so old and so dead they couldn't even tell
what it was or had been. So now I'm telling you—
hundreds of millions of years ago that rock was

a living thing, as was my father when he found it.
That's my show and tell contribution. These thoughts
and feelings may be extinct in me now but
I've written them down to prove they once lived.

THE SMOOTH DREAMER

it is unknown whether
the smooth dreamer dreams
or even if she sleeps
three thousand feet below
the surface of the sea
almost motionlessly she floats
only a slim band of light
beckons from her brow line
attracting prey and mates
it resembles a windshield wiper
her lifespan is unknown
her fin-care routine is unknown
unknown is her opinion
of ahi tuna's popularity
whether she knows we call her
the ugliest known creature
is unknown but I suspect
she's been too busy
with those six boyfriends
flocking her constantly
they say they want to live
inside her look how
they've shrivelled up
become parasites
when those sorry guys
claimed they'd die for her
they weren't lying

THE SADNESS OF MARGE SIMPSON

There's a coffee stain
in my copy of Dean Young's *Selected Poems*
that looks like Marge Simpson in a windstorm.
I stare at this stain while not reading
a single Dean Young poem,
holding the book on my lap,
hoping something will happen.
What do I hope for? That all of the law schools
I've never applied to will admit me,
and that my dad didn't actually die
but has been in China this whole time
gawking at the Great Wall like he always wanted
and maybe Marge Simpson is with him,
having finally divorced her declining franchise.
What actually happens: the mail carrier
slips the two chapbooks I ordered off the internet
through the slot in my door. They land
with a whoosh on my fake-wood floor.
I open them and say, *Hello,*
strangers. Let's get wrecked.
Recently I've been sad, so I moved
to this island. It's nice, if a little quiet,
and I'm still sad. You can run all your life
into new lives but sadness is an episodic bitch.
You can star on *The Simpsons* and *Mmmm*
the same *Mmmm* for thirty years.
One of the chapbooks I received was me
and the other chapbook was Marge Simpson,
but both chapbooks were sad.
Sadness is a lacy French maiden name
buried alive under Simpson.
Sadness has the same absence of friends
as Marge Simpson, the same memorability.
Sadness is writing this poem

while Dean Young was alive, editing it after he died,
and deciding to book him on the same tour bus
as Marge and my father. His original heart
holds open the guidebook.
Sadness is a mouse that kills a cat
over and over with his trunk of endless props.
One chapbook is called *Itchy*.
The second chapbook is *Scratchy*.
One chapbook will win prizes
and one chapbook be remaindered.
Your husband laughs. Your kids laugh.
You laugh, too, your sad throaty laugh.
Sadness is a show within a show,
a poem inside a poem. It gets you
to the sofa and dictates how you sit on it.
I open a box labelled *plates* and find plates,
but between each of them is the sadness
I forgot I wrapped them in.
Grief is like that, I'm learning.
I packed my dad's urn in a box with plastic cactuses
and laughed when I found it. I wrote
a chapbook called *The Lost Daughter*
and a chapbook called *Famous Monsters*
and a chapbook called *The Sadness of Marge Simpson*
and a chapbook called *I'm Sorry I Left
Without Saying Goodbye to Anyone*—
but no one would publish *I'm Sorry I Left
Without Saying Goodbye to Anyone*.
My new apartment in my new life
has enough cupboards for me to hide
certain things from myself, at least for a while.
Oh, Dean Young, you were so goofy
you thought we couldn't see through
to your sloshing human moods.
Marge Simpson's impossible tower of hair
isn't fooling anyone either—
the only truth is its blue.

FREEDOM

Yesterday my student told me he'd like to write
about a woman's breast he glimpsed
while sitting on the beach and I don't know
how to advise him. My wife thinks
I should insist I'm the wrong advisor
for his project—I hardly write
about the body and often forget I even have one.
This morning, petting my cat's belly,
I was very aware of her many nipples.
Small spayed creature, she'll never need them
and sometimes they make me feel weird.
My student, who's in his seventies, writes
gentle poems about many things—
his dead friends and relatives, seagulls and roses—
and now breasts are what interest him most.
Going up and down the deli aisle
with my wife, breasts under our shirts
and breasts in a basket between us,
I thought of those huge mammary clouds
we stood under in Portland our second
Valentine's Day together—braless
they drifted, feeding the Pearl District.
I want to tell my student he is free to write
about breasts because he is. All of us are free.
But haven't breasts launched enough
ships into the creepy sea of literature?
Still, I believe poetry can help people
create meaning from their experiences—
it's why I teach—and my student
experiences breasts. *I don't want everyone
thinking I'm some dirty old man,* he says.
I tell him to put that in his poem
and try to help him with the rest.

FATHER CHRISTMAS

Whenever anyone's rental Santa cancelled
your father was called to stand in.
Solemnly he donned the red pyjamas and drove off
to rescue that other family's Christmas.
Everyone knows a man who resembles
your father: milk-white hair,
red cheeks, proverbial jelly bowl.
Even if you haven't caught him in your chimney
you've seen him on commercials and cookie tins,
know his affinity for unorthodox pets.
But you've also seen him muttering to himself
as he pushes a shopping cart up your alley—
this time his black sack is full of trash
instead of presents, bottles
he'll exchange for lottery tickets and cans
he'll cash into mickeys of R&R
There are two sorts of Santas in the world,
your father taught you, one on the nice list
and one on the naughty. One Santa
has a solid support system and the other
plunges through claymation clouds.
One Santa got the job, married the girl,
bought the two-car garage while the other Santa
sawed off his shotgun. One Santa
got everything and still sawed off his shotgun,
his brain chemistry the naughty Santa.
One Santa filled his basement with model trains.
One Santa filled his pain pill prescription
and kept filling and taking and filling and taking
but the pain wouldn't go away
until he went away as well. The other Santa
plays ukulele in swim trunks. One Santa was
born in this country and one Santa wasn't.

You saw one Santa on a park bench training
an army of ducks with Wonder Bread and another
conducting the London Symphony Orchestra.
Florida Santa was arrested for possession.
One Santa was voted into office
where many previous Santas have served,
their portraits wallpapering an austere hallway.
By now you've mixed up the Santas—naughty,
nice, naughty, nice—forgotten which is which.
That's ok. You're not supposed to know.
That information is Santa's and he has it on a list.
What's important is that all of the Santas, Santas
on both sides, just want to give you gifts—
that's the mission they've been given.
They want to sit you on their knee.
They want to listen to your wishes.
They want to answer your annual letters,
to hear how you've helped your mom,
aced your exams, and are going to be a doctor.
When your father comes home, there will be
two of him, the original and the understudy—
one lucky and the other unlucky—
and they'll linger a while in the driveway
clutching cups of cheer, the cigarette smoke
swirling up around their faces
like second beards. They'll laugh
at some dad joke—their jelly bowls jiggling
like jelly bowls, their cheeks going
from candy apple to cranberry—
and you won't be able to tell them apart,
they look so similar you've mixed them up,
forgotten which Santa you're mad at
and which is the one you're supposed to love.

STATIC

I suspect my grocery store cactus
is made of plastic. For years it's sat
on my desk and I've watered it occasionally
and forgotten about it regularly.
It hasn't grown or changed colour.
It hasn't leaned, hasn't flowered.
It hasn't shrivelled like a bellybutton.
Unlike my Norfolk pine and spider plant
it hasn't suffered failures of confidence;
I haven't coaxed it back from that edge.
It hasn't taken a gap year in France
and only tells me to go fuck myself
when I touch it. It hasn't stood weeping
in the bathtub with Frank O'Hara.
Mother, how many decades did you
spend waiting for something to change?
Then you died, so I suppose finally
something did. The television threw
shadows, complex weather patterns
across your face, and the television
blathered on and on like a friend.

DAD POEM

Once, my father mailed me a poem
he'd written during the period breaks
of a Flames game—rhyming quatrains
printed neatly on looseleaf.
Rereading it recently, I didn't notice
the quality of his words, only
how the paper was like a rectangle of light
cast inside some dusty attic
by a south-facing window, so bright
I could hardly decipher it.
With my left hand, I lifted the page
and dangled it out to one side
for a few moments
as though it was a SAD lamp
dimming my inner winter.
When I reached my right hand out
to touch it, my fingertips sunk
through the page. I inched it
over my hand and wrist.
Soon I was in up to my elbow.
Holding my breath, I plunged my bicep
and when I looked behind the page
only the back side was visible—
the straight blue lines and three
neat holes like the spinal column
of some important constellation.
I didn't know what to do next
so I withdrew my arm.
Confident I was unharmed,
I set the page on the floor
and stepped gently onto it
as if onto a scale. Several
seconds slid into the past.

Then the room flickered like a channel
changing on an old TV
and I was no longer standing
in my bedroom. Suddenly
I remembered my father's poem.
Remembered isn't quite
the way to say it. Instead, his words
sort of whooshed through me
like a bunch of kids
barrelling down a country road
in their parents' Buick.
On the ceiling, the poem
was blaring its clinical-strength light
and I was standing my parents' basement.
You can lose your life
in memories, my father wrote
in his poem, imperfectly rhyming
memories with *tenderly*,
and there he was behind me,
sinking into our old sofa
like a brontosaurus into a tarpit.
Quit blocking the screen,
he said, waving a hand.
Settling into my old spot
on the love seat, I put my feet up.
Same glass-top coffee tables
crusted with gunk. Same ancient
carpets. Same bowling trophy
with its same golden man frozen
mid-throw. The only difference
was the poem on the coffee table
in front of him, the one
he'd mailed to me. But the poem
I'd come in through
was still stuck to the ceiling,
so there were now two poems—

which presented a dilemma, as I knew
I'd need to go through one of them
to get back into my life.
Both poems were glowing.
I thought back on my English degree
for something that might help me
navigate the situation.
I thought of Robert Frost,
though neither poem looked
particularly travelled by.
Wallace Stevens might
have an opinion, but I wouldn't
understand it even if I could
remember anything he'd written.
Smoke doodled on the air
as my father's cigarette
disintegrated in its crystal ashtray.
Do you know which poem
I should take? I asked him
during a commercial break.
You know, he said, *we all*
used to hitchhike. This was
the seventies mind you
but it was totally safe
and normal. Even I would
pick people up sometimes
if I was having trouble
staying awake at the wheel.
When he had finished speaking,
both poems began to glow
significantly brighter,
as if an invisible finger
was pushing up the dimmer.
It was difficult at this point
to see the television,
though my father

appeared not to notice.
The poems were also
getting larger and had already
grown into legal-sized documents.
I had the sense I needed
to choose soon before they
overtook the whole room.
But I wanted to stay
in that basement forever.
I squinted at my father.
It was so hard to see him
with these stupid poems
casting all their unhelpful light.
I understood then what he meant
about hitchhiking
and about staying awake.
Standing up, I squeezed his foot
through the afghan and told him
I'd see him later.
Then I got into the poem—
it doesn't matter which poem—
and let it take me
wherever it was going.

PRODUCE

When I was twenty-two and miserable
I would bike to The Root Cellar
and wander through the stacks of produce
imagining they were famous works

in a gallery. *Radishes* by Cézanne.
The Great Mountain of Zucchini by Hokusai.
Georgia O'Keeffe's *Purple Cabbage*.
It helped to be alone among vegetables

those dim mushroomy afternoons
within the potato's ancient silence,
the acorn squash hush, and the excited
quiet of bunched kale. I was hardly

even offended when a clerk insisted
I'd pronounced Swiss chard wrong.
Of similarly low importance: the life
I'd been growing of shitty poems,

breakups, and long, anxious hangovers.
I realize now I didn't need to imagine,
the vegetables were already art—
someone had created them out of dirt

and someone else had selected them.
Someone stickered their sides.
Someone packed and drove them
to town where another someone

in a simple red shirt and black apron
stacked them into the towers and rows
I could reach out and touch,
taking all I needed to sustain me.

When you visit your father in the underworld, do not take a candy from the crystal bowl on his coffee table.

When you visit your father in the underworld, do not take a candy from the crystal bowl on his coffee table, and do not watch reruns of *Law & Order*.

When you visit your father in the underworld, do not take a candy from the crystal bowl on his coffee table, do not watch reruns of *Law & Order*, and do not leave your shadow in his bathtub.

When you visit your father in the underworld, do not take a candy from the crystal bowl on his coffee table, do not watch reruns of *Law & Order*, do not leave your shadow in his bathtub, and do not count the bunnies on the pilsner bottles.

When you visit your father in the underworld, do not take a candy from the crystal bowl on his coffee table, do not watch reruns of *Law & Order*, do not leave your shadow in his bathtub, do not count the bunnies on the pilsner bottles, and do not yawn.

When you visit your father in the underworld, do not take a candy from the crystal bowl on his coffee table, do not watch reruns of *Law & Order*, do not leave your shadow in his bathtub, do not count the bunnies on the pilsner bottles, do not yawn, and do not ask the river of blood what your name is.

When you visit your father in the underworld, do not take a candy from the crystal bowl on his coffee table, do not watch reruns of *Law & Order*, do not leave your shadow in his bathtub, do not count the bunnies on the pilsner bottles, do not yawn, do not ask the river of blood what your name is, and under no circumstances go bowling.

When you visit your father in the underworld, do not take a candy from the crystal bowl on his coffee table, do not watch reruns of *Law & Order*, do not leave your shadow in his bathtub, do not count the bunnies on the pilsner bottles, do not yawn, do not ask the river of blood what your name is, under no circumstances go bowling, and do not let the crows breakfast on your hemorrhoids.

When you visit your father in the underworld, do not take a candy from the crystal bowl on his coffee table, do not watch reruns of *Law & Order*, do not leave your shadow in his bathtub, do not count the bunnies on the pilsner bottles, do not yawn, do not ask the river of blood what your name is, under no circumstances go bowling, do not let the crows breakfast on your hemorrhoids, and do not make eye contact with the owls.

When you visit your father in the underworld, do not take a candy from the crystal bowl on his coffee table, do not watch reruns of *Law & Order*, do not leave your shadow in his bathtub, do not count the bunnies on the pilsner bottles, do not yawn, do not ask the river of blood what your name is, under no circumstances go bowling, do not let the crows breakfast on your hemorrhoids, do not make eye contact with the owls, and do not ask him to come home with you, and do not ask if you can stay.

POLYP

Since his diagnosis, my father-in-law thinks
everyone has nasal polyps. His daughters. His dog,
His phlegmy priest. And now me.

At the dinner table, he angles his soup spoon
for a view, then volunteers to teach me the waltz
just so he can tip me way back. Polyp:

a rogue growth. Cellular excess. A flesh curdle—
akin to the spider I found crumpled
in a library copy of *Paradise Lost* or the proverbial

gum wad thumbed onto the underside of anything.
Among the rooms of his big suburban home,
my father-in-law wanders. King of the corner lot.

Baron of looking important before a barbecue
but now he's got these teardrop-shaped errors
inside his face and maybe they've always been there,

maybe they're everywhere. He touches a succulent
on a windowsill and whispers, *Polyp.*
He touches the Last Supper his wife cross-stitched,

lets a finger rest on Judas's left foot. He moves along
to the dishwasher. The garburator switch. His daughters'
graduation portraits. The sun-warmed spot

on his bedspread. His chin, its reflection
in the master bath mirror. *Polyp*, whispers
my father-in-law. *Polyp. Polyp. Polyp.*

We empty the litter boxes.
Give the old cat her medicine
and watch the young one
hack up another hairball.
I do dishes. You complain
about your day. We listen
to our drunk neighbours
and pray they don't set
the building on fire again.
We argue over where to go
for dinner and whether
we've gone out too much
lately. It doesn't feel
like it's been seven years—
this, us. Seven springs,
seven summers, seven
competitive pumpkins,
seven mildewy winters.
And yet my parents are
both gone now and your
grandmother. We've been
granted three nephews,
three kid-shaped fountains
of pirate games and chaos.
You drive us to the beach
in our good old beater.
Fading in the twilight,
the sky is still there.
The water sits under it,
still moody and refusing
to settle down. The sand
that gets in everything
still gets in everything.
You're here. You get it.

BAGGAGE

On top of the suitcase my father carried to Canada
I prop up my iPad for video classes with my students.
Because it isn't tall enough for a good camera angle
I stack a few textbooks on top of it. The suitcase
my father carried to Canada is the size of a large shoebox,
like the one my Chelsea boots came in. It is brown
with metal rivets. It would make an excellent coffin
for a small cat. On the suitcase my father carried
to Canada, on textbooks he paid for, I tell my students
about metaphors and line breaks. I tell them to find
the stakes, by which I maybe mean the inner suitcase
of the poem. Like, if the poem was six years old
and had to flee the country with its mother at dusk,
what would it take with it? Trick question: a poem
never packs its own suitcase, its mother does.
My students are mostly kind. They listen They want
magazines to publish them. The suitcase my father
carried to Canada listens in on my classes, but I won't
tell my students about it. They don't need to know
what their class is conducted on. I rub the metal handle
whenever I don't know what to say. I fiddle with
the latches. My father came to Canada. I write poems.
The suitcase he carried is my heaviest textbook.

COHO

Whenever I'm sad, I lift my fish book
off the shelf and let it fall open in my lap.
Today I got coho. I would've liked an eel
or even a smelt but I only get one flip.
That's the game: one feeling, one flip.
Years ago, my father and I caught a salmon
so small we assumed we'd hooked weeds—
the bell he clipped to the tip of his rod
barely rattled. When we finally reeled in
there it was at the end of our line, limp
and tiny, like an infant's filthy sock.
My father knelt down at the river's edge
to unhook it. Cupping it in his palms,
he said, "I dunno. Might not make it."
Each syllable came out with a little cloud.
Then the fish swam away. I wish it would
let me go, this feeling, but I like its warm
hands, the way it wears my father's face.

THIRTEEN YEARS

I never believed the story you told me about the girl
who came into the bookstore you worked at
and then drowned herself in the ocean a few days later.

You said you'd avoided her pretty, desperate face
in the aisles, had jokingly recommended *Mrs. Dalloway*
when she cornered you for books about dying.

The girl, Virginia Woolf, stones in both their pockets—
it fit too well together. I assumed you were trying
to tell me about yourself but had to use the girl to do it.

That fall, you wrote a poem about the tide bearing her
away like a bottle with a note curled up inside it.
Our writing group loved that poem. I loved it too,

even if I didn't believe it. At the time, I wrote tiny poems,
stripped to nouns and verbs, a kind of writing
someone might admire but never love.

We drank wine on beaches, then waded in.
When water weighed down our tights, we tied them
around our necks, sliced our bare feet on stones.

Years later, I asked what had happened
to that poem and you told me you'd tried editing it,
but every line was bad. Every line? I doubted that

the way I doubted the story itself and the others
you've told before and since, brimming with coincidence,
characters resurfacing as if in an epic novel.

We live in separate cities now. Hundreds of people
like the filtered images you share of your life
while I post fewer and fewer photos. We've been friends

for thirteen years and I don't know how many times
you've wanted to die. I want you to tell me this fact,
awful as a body hauled in on the tide. Tell me the story

you started years ago, about being cornered by yourself
and laughing your way out of it. Maybe it's me
who needs passing encounters to mean something,

who can't just let stories squawk from far-off rocks.
For thirteen years you've told me I'm too honest
and I know you're right. I go to the beach

to watch the ocean's great grey breathing
and wonder which stones you would choose,
knowing they'd be identical to my own.

WINNING

One summer, my father and I ate our way
through dozens of boxes of popsicles
so that he could construct a catapult
for a town competition. Our mouths went blue,
orange, purple, red with his hunger to win.
He loved that brief epoch when you could peel
the plastic out of bottle caps and win something
instantly. Packing our pantry with flats of pop
he didn't like, he often had *Better Luck*
Next Time. On holidays, he booked hotels
attached to casinos, disappeared for so long
after dinner I fell asleep with the TV.
When I woke up, he'd be on the second bed
watching Sportsnet. He rolled up the rims,
filled out entry forms at grocery stores
for everyone in the family. A magician
at hockey games—from his pockets he pulled
endless handkerchiefs of fifty-fifty tickets.
I could count on my Christmas stocking
to be stuffed full of scratch'n'wins.
Thursday nights were for Texas Hold'em.
After he died, I found a stack of Lotto Max
half an inch thick. Posthumously he won
seventeen dollars and a free play.
Otherwise his wallet was empty.

I'm done with happiness. I don't want to watch a sunset
or open myself up to the universe's secret handshakes.
I refuse to coo. I won't babble with strangers
on sidewalks about the blooming neighbourhood
or go bowling and be ok coming in last because I'm just there
for the fun of it—I'm never just there for the fun of it.
I'm done letting mall hippies sell me chakras
and oregano oil. I will no longer be signing-off emails
Warmly or *Best*. If I buy your chocolate almonds,
don't think it's because I care about your summer camp.
I just don't feel separate-yet-connected like a cog
in the we're-all-in-this-together clock. I'm sick of people
smugly gifting me tomatoes from their gardens,
but not as sick as I am of toddlers befriending
farm animals or celebrities singing "Imagine" together
through the webcams in their separate mansions. No,
I don't have a minute to talk about children's literacy.
I resent your affirmations and your aromatherapy stinks.
No matter how many stock images suggest otherwise,
salad never was a good stand-up comedian. Go
plug your mantras into someone else's energy field.
Guzzle your own green juice, Sharon, for I'm done
retrofitting my regrets into ten-part PG miniserieses
starring Michael Cera and Emma Stone. I'm chopping
up my vision board for kindling. I'm setting
my vision kindling on fire with my hot hot hatred
of college kids hanging prayer flags from their balconies.
I just want to sit in a lawn chair next to my toxic fire
solo-drinking like the baron of private property signs
until I drunk-dial sadness to tell her that I love her,
that it's her I've loved all along, her voice
I long to hear, reminding me I'm going to die too,
as she slides her midnight-cold toes up my shins.

Those slow green afternoons at the river, I watched my father kill fish with a hatchet and one quick whack. I watched him kill their bodies with a long, thin blade. He killed mosquitoes with his palms. Cigarettes he killed with his breath, finished them off in beer cans and in sand. He killed the breeze with the door crank. He killed the engine, which killed the radio and the outing. One summer, he killed the slugs with beer and a plastic frisbee. He killed beer, serially. He killed teenaged pine trees so that my mother and I could wrap their corpses in lights and crap. Passively and with cliché traps, he killed the pantry mice. With a flashlight and a wire hanger, he killed the under-the-bed monsters. The spines of Western paperbacks. The soles of Fields sandals. The lights. He killed my questions with his answers. My hunger with meatloaf and Kraft Dinner. He killed the badger that had been killing his chickens. Then he killed his chickens. The moss. The dandelions. The crab grass. The television with the remote. Silence with the remote. Closeness with the remote. Poker. Five at a time, he killed the pins at the end of the waxed runway. He killed a squirrel with his truck. A porcupine with his truck. His truck with a moose. Kicking down the door, he killed the possibility my grandfather was still living. He killed ice with salt. Mould with bleach. Dirt with the washing machine. You already know the last thing he killed, with pills and neglect. I shouldn't have to say it.

ACKNOWLEDGEMENTS

Poems from this collection previously appeared in *The Fiddlehead, The New Quarterly, CV2, Riddle Fence, Queer Little Nightmares: An Anthology of Monstrous Fiction and Poetry, The Walrus, Vallum, Maisonneuve,* ARC *Poetry Magazine, long con, The Antigonish Review, The Malahat Review,* PRISM *international, Grain,* and *Room Magazine.* Thank you to all the editors who made space for my work.

Thank you Souvankham Thammavongsa for selecting "The Peace Lily" for *Best Canadian Poetry in English 2021* and Bardia Sinaee for choosing "Thirteen Years" for *Best Canadian Poetry in English 2024.*

For edits and support with early drafts, thank you Rob Taylor, Shaun Robinson, and the Sunroom Poets. For sitting across tables and laptop screens and writing with me, thank you Jessie Jones, Nadine Bachan, and André Babyn.

Thank you Kevin Connolly for coaching me through this one—phew, we made it! And so much gratitude to the rest of the team at House of Anansi Press for your care and support.

Thank you to the Canada Council for the Arts for helping pay the bills.

Thank you to my wife, Angela, for listening to hundreds of bad drafts and for sticking around, through everything.

PHOTO BY ERIN FLEGG

KAYLA CZAGA is the author of two previous poetry collections—
For Your Safety Please Hold On (Nightwood Editions, 2014), and
Dunk Tank (House of Anansi, 2019). Her work has been short-
listed for the Governor General's Award for poetry and the BC
and Yukon Book Prizes' Dorothy Livesay Poetry Prize. Frequently
anthologized in the *Best Canadian Poetry in English* series, her
writing has also appeared in *The Walrus, Grain, Event, The
Fiddlehead,* and elsewhere. She lives with her wife on the tradi-
tional territory of the Lekwungen people, the Songhees and
Esquimalt nations.